DOWNSIDE OF DRUGS

Hard Drugs

Cocaine, LSD, PCP, & Heroin

DOWNSIDE of DRUGS

DOWNSIDE OF DRUGS

Hard Drugs
Cocaine, LSD, PCP, & Heroin

Celicia Scott

Mason Crest

Mason Crest
450 Parkway Drive, Suite D
Broomall, PA 19008
www.masoncrest.com

Printed and bound in the United States of America.

9 8 7 6 5 4 3 2

Series ISBN: 978-1-4222-3015-2
ISBN: 978-1-4222-3021-3
ebook ISBN: 978-1-4222-8807-8

Cataloging-in-Publication Data on file with the Library of Congress.

Contents

INTRODUCTION

One of the best parts of getting older is the opportunity to make your own choices. As your parents give you more space and you spend more time with friends than family, you are called upon to make more decisions for yourself. Many important decisions that present themselves in the teen years may change your life. The people with whom you are friendly, how much effort you put into school and other activities, and what kinds of experiences you choose for yourself all affect the person you will become as you emerge from being a child into becoming a young adult.

One of the most important decisions you will make is whether or not you use substances like alcohol, marijuana, crystal meth, and cocaine. Even using prescription medicines incorrectly or relying on caffeine to get through your daily life can shape your life today and your future tomorrow. These decisions can impact all the other decisions you make. If you decide to say yes to drug abuse, the impact on your life is usually not a good one!

One suggestion I make to many of my patients is this: think about how you will respond to an offer to use drugs before it happens. In the heat of the moment, particularly if you're feeling some peer pressure, it can be hard to think clearly—so be prepared ahead of time. Thinking about why you don't want to use drugs and how you'll respond if you are asked to use them can make it easier to make a healthy decision when the time comes. Just like practicing a sport makes it easier to play in a big game, having thought about why drugs aren't a good fit for you and exactly what you might say to avoid them can give you the "practice" you need to do what's best for you. It can make a tough situation simpler once it arises.

In addition, talk about drugs with your parents or a trusted adult. This will both give you support and help you clarify your thinking. The decision is still yours to make, but adults can be a good resource. Take advantage of the information and help they can offer you.

Sometimes, young people fall into abusing drugs without really thinking about it ahead of time. It can sometimes be hard to recognize when you're making a decision that might hurt you. You might be with a friend or acquaintance in a situation that feels comfortable. There may be things in your life that are hard, and it could seem like using drugs might make them easier. It's also natural to be curious about new experiences. However, by not making a decision ahead of time, you may be actually making a decision without realizing it, one that will limit your choices in the future.

When someone offers you drugs, there is no flashing sign that says, "Hey, think about what you're doing!" Making a good decision may be harder because the "fun" part happens immediately while the downside—the damage to your brain and the rest of your body—may not be obvious right away. One of the biggest downsides of drugs is that they have long-term effects on your life. They could reduce your educational, career, and relationship opportunities. Drug use often leaves users with more problems than when they started.

Whenever you make a decision, it's important to know all the facts. When it comes to drugs, you'll need answers to questions like these: How do different drugs work? Is there any "safe" way to use drugs? How will drugs hurt my body and my brain? If I don't notice any bad effects right away, does that mean these drugs are safe? Are these drugs addictive? What are the legal consequences of using drugs? This book discusses these questions and helps give you the facts to make good decisions.

Reading this book is a great way to start, but if you still have questions, keep looking for the answers. There is a lot of information on the Internet, but not all of it is reliable. At the back of this book, you'll find a list of more books and good websites for finding out more about this drug. A good website is teens.drugabuse.gov, a site compiled for teens by the National Institute on Drug Abuse (NIDA). This is a reputable federal government agency that researches substance use and how to prevent it. This website does a good job looking at a lot of data and consolidating it into easy-to-understand messages.

What if you are worried you already have a problem with drugs? If that's the case, the best thing to do is talk to your doctor or another trusted adult to help figure out what to do next. They can help you find a place to get treatment.

Drugs have a downside—but as a young adult, you have the power to make decisions for yourself about what's best for you. Use your power wisely!

—Joshua Borus, MD

1. WHAT ARE HARD DRUGS?

All drugs are chemicals that change the way your body works in some way. Drugs can be medicines that control pain or cure diseases. But drugs can also be dangerous substances. People may use them for recreation—but they're a risky way to have a good time.

Hard drugs are drugs that have serious and dangerous physical consequences. Most hard drugs are illegal. Hard drugs have a very big downside!

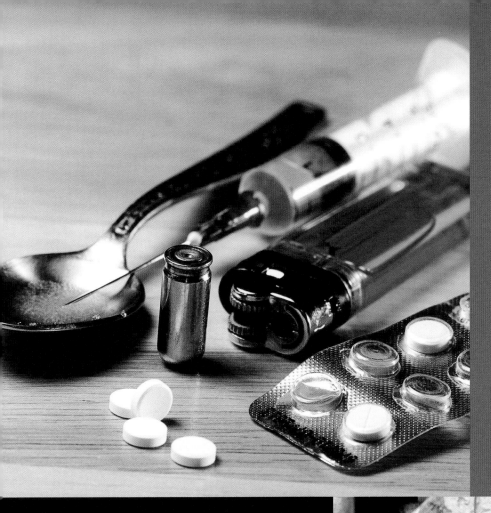

Examples of hard drugs:

- cocaine
- LSD
- PCP
- heroin

Other hard drugs are methamphetamine (meth), alcohol, and nicotine. Even though alcohol and nicotine are legal, they are still very dangerous. Governments often put taxes on their sale to regulate their use. They also have laws in place to prevent children and young adults from using them.

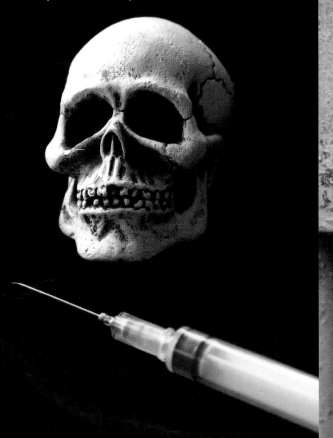

Using hard drugs can make you very sick. They could even kill you.

Using hard drugs is a crime that could land you in prison.

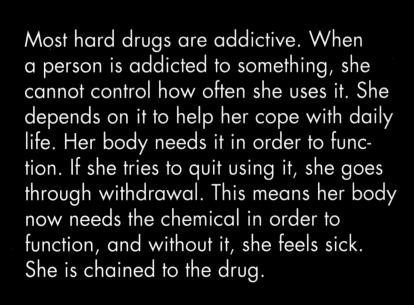

2. WHAT ARE THE DOWNSIDES OF THESE DRUGS?

Most hard drugs are addictive. When a person is addicted to something, she cannot control how often she uses it. She depends on it to help her cope with daily life. Her body needs it in order to function. If she tries to quit using it, she goes through withdrawal. This means her body now needs the chemical in order to function, and without it, she feels sick. She is chained to the drug.

After using cocaine regularly over a long period, dependence (addiction) develops. Stopping cocaine now will cause withdrawal. Cocaine withdrawal *symptoms* include:

- *depression* and *anxiety*
- extreme tiredness
- difficulty concentrating
- losing the ability to feel pleasure
- aches, pains, *tremors*, and chills

Withdrawal symptoms from cocaine addiction usually go away within one to two weeks. However, intense craving for cocaine may return, even years after the last use.

Heroin is extremely addictive. People who use heroin regularly may go through withdrawal even if they go without heroin for only a few hours. Withdrawal symptoms from heroin include:

- muscle and bone pain
- restlessness
- *insomnia*
- cold flashes and goose bumps
- diarrhea and vomiting

Withdrawal symptoms from heroin usually get better after about a week.

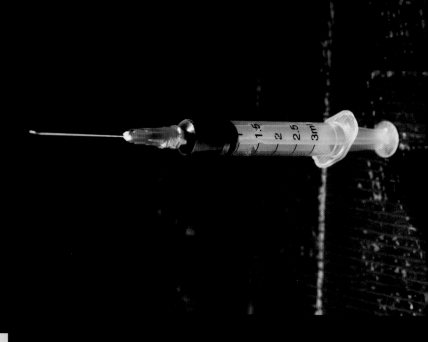

Although LSD does not cause addiction, it does have other various serious effects on the brain, some of which may be permanent.

PCP causes addiction. Withdrawal symptoms include diarrhea, chills, and tremors.

3. WHAT IS COCAINE?

Cocaine comes from the leaves of the coca bush, a plant that grows in the Andes Mountains in South America. Different chemical processes produce the two main forms of cocaine:

- powdered cocaine, often known as "coke" or "blow"
- crack cocaine, also known as "rock"

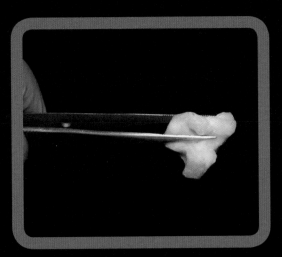

Users snort powdered cocaine into their noses—or they dissolve it in water and inject it into their blood with needles.

Crack cocaine is smoked in small pipes like this one.

No matter how cocaine is taken, it's dangerous. At first, a person who takes cocaine might feel full of energy, happy, and excited. But then his mood can change, and he may become angry, nervous, and afraid that someone's out to get him. He might do things that make no sense. After the "high" is over, he can "crash" and feel tired and sad for days. This may give him a strong craving to take the drug again to try to feel better.

4. WHAT IS LSD?

LSD is one of the strongest mood-changing drugs. The drug is manufactured in crystal form in illegal labs, mainly in the United States. These crystals are then put in a liquid that is odorless, colorless, and has a slightly bitter taste. The liquid can then be sold in small tablets (called "microdots" or "dots"), capsules, or gelatin squares (called "window panes"). LSD is also known as "acid" and by many other names, including "doses" and "trips."

LSD comes from lysergic acid, which is found in a fungus called ergot that grows on rye and other grains.

Getting high on LSD is called a "trip." It typically lasts about twelve hours. When things go wrong, which often happens, it is called a "bad trip." Bad trips can be terrifying experiences!

Often, LSD is added to absorbent paper (referred to as "blotters"), which is then divided into small squares.

Blotters are often decorated with designs or cartoon characters. (This form of LSD is sometimes called Loony Tunes.)

No matter what form it comes in, LSD changes the way users see reality. It makes them see a world that looks very different from the way things normally look.

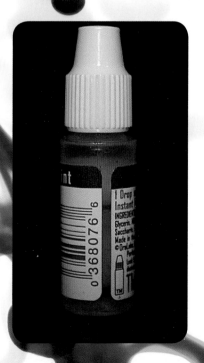

Once in a while, LSD is sold in liquid form.

PCP's real name is phencyclidine. It was originally created in the 1950s by scientists as a drug to be used for *anesthesia* during surgery. Doctors stopped using it in 1965 because they found that patients often became upset, *irrational*, and *delusional* when they were recovering from the effects of PCP. But some people kept using PCP illegally. Today, its street names are Angel Dust, Embalming Fluid, Ozone, Rocket Fuel, Wack, and Killer Weed.

People who use PCP feel as though they're having "out-of-body" experiences. They feel cut off from reality.

PCP is a white powder that can be dissolved in water. It has a bitter taste. It is sold illegally as tablets, capsules, and colored powders. It can be snorted, smoked, injected with a needle, or swallowed. It may be wrapped in foil packets like the ones show here, and it's also often applied to mint leaves, tobacco, or marijuana leaves.

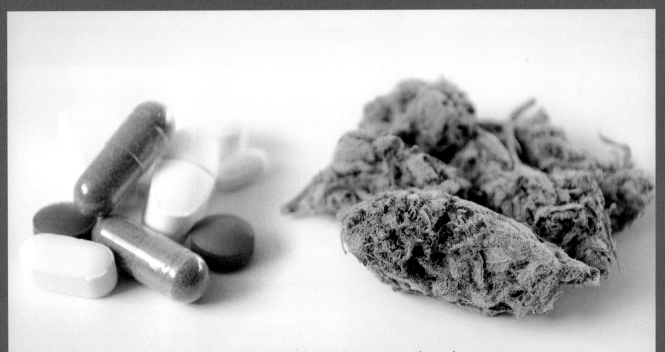

Sometimes people use PCP without knowing that they are, since it's often added to marijuana, LSD, or methamphetamine.

0. WHAT IS HEROIN?

Heroin is a very dangerous hard drug that's a white or brown powder. It can also be a black, sticky substance. (This kind is called "black tar" heroin.) Other names for heroin are dope, big H, Dr. Feelgood, smack, horse, black tar, junk, mud, skag, and brown sugar. Smoking heroin is sometimes referred to as "chasing the dragon."

Heroin is made from morphine, a drug that comes from opium poppies.

Heroin was first created to be a painkiller and a cough medicine. The same company that now makes Bayer Aspirin sold "Heroin" at the end of the nineteenth century. The company didn't know yet how dangerous the drug would be!

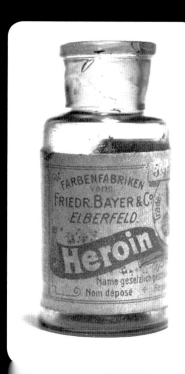

When you take heroin, you can never be quite sure what you're taking, since it is often mixed with other drugs or substances, such as sugar or powdered milk. It may also be mixed with poisons, such as strychnine.

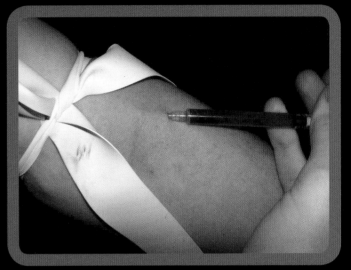

Heroin can be used in several different ways. It can be put into a person's blood with a needle, which is called "mainlining," or it can be injected into a muscle.

It can be smoked, either in a pipe or mixed in a marijuana joint or a regular cigarette.

It can also be inhaled as smoke through a straw or snorted as powder into the nose.

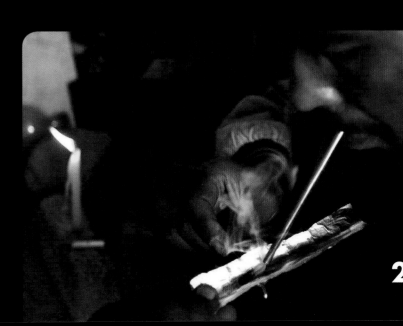

7. WHAT HAPPENS TO YOUR BODY WHEN YOU USE COCAINE?

Once cocaine enters a person's body, it travels through the blood and affects the entire body. It harms the brain, the heart, the blood vessels, and the lungs. It's so dangerous that it's the reason for more emergency room visits in the United States than any other illegal drug.

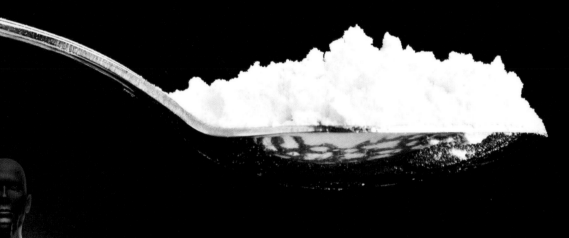

Cocaine is bad for a person's heart. Cocaine increases heart rate and blood pressure. It makes the arteries that bring blood to the heart become narrower and smaller. This can cause a heart attack—even in young people who have nothing wrong with their hearts otherwise. Cocaine can also make the heart's rhythm become unsteady, going first too fast and then too slow.

Cocaine also narrows the blood vessels inside the brain. This can cause a *stroke*, even in young people. Cocaine also causes *seizures*.

When people snort cocaine, they can damage their noses and sinuses. Regular cocaine use can put holes in the nasal passageways.

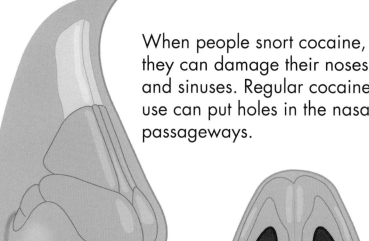

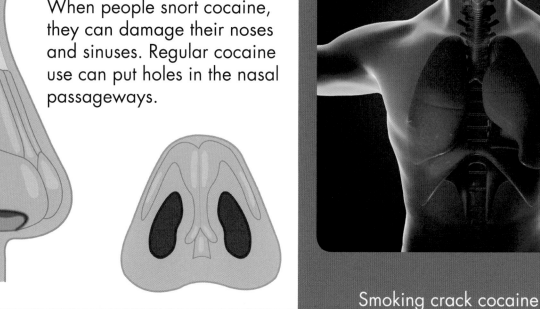

Smoking crack cocaine *irritates* the lungs. In some people, it causes permanent lung damage.

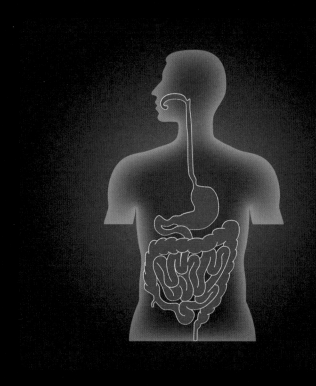

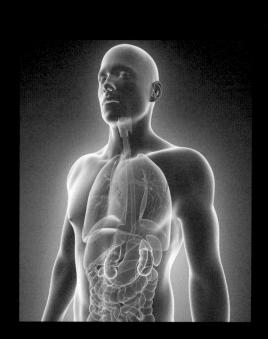

Cocaine also narrows the blood vessels that bring blood to the stomach and intestines. When the stomach and intestines don't get the blood they need, their cells don't have enough oxygen. This can cause ulcers. Sometime, this can also put holes in the stomach wall or in the intestines.

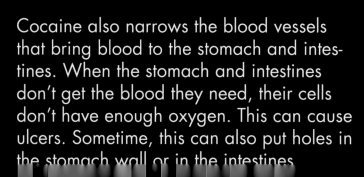

Cocaine can cause sudden kidney failure. People need their kidneys to remove wastes from their bodies. If their kidneys don't do their jobs, people die.

8. WHAT HAPPENS TO YOUR BODY WHEN YOU USE LSD?

LSD affects your brain—but it also affects the rest of your body.

- If you're using LSD, you may have a fever.
- Your blood pressure will increase.
- Your heart will beat faster.
- Your muscles will feel weak and shaky; they may even lose feeling.
- Your pupils will get get larger.
- Your mouth will feel dry.
- You'll feel sweaty.
- You may feel sick to your stomach.

Physical effects of
Lysergic acid diethylamide (LSD)

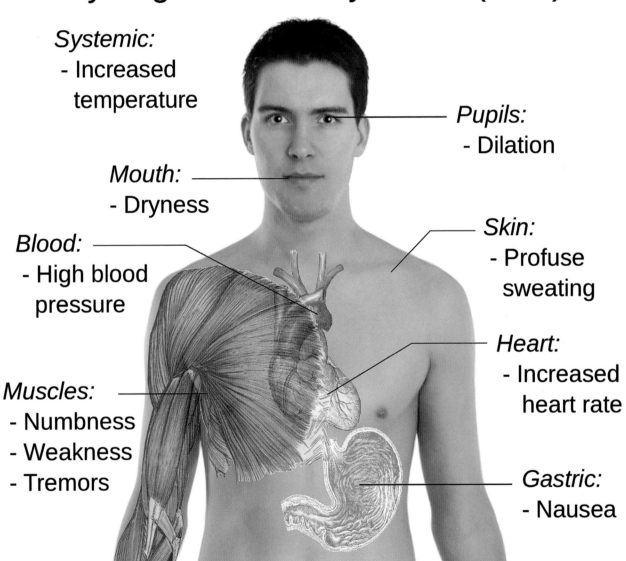

Systemic:
- Increased temperature

Pupils:
- Dilation

Mouth:
- Dryness

Skin:
- Profuse sweating

Blood:
- High blood pressure

Heart:
- Increased heart rate

Muscles:
- Numbness
- Weakness
- Tremors

Gastric:
- Nausea

9. WHAT HAPPENS TO YOUR BODY WHEN YOU USE PCP?

When people take smaller doses of PCP, the effects on their bodies are similar to what they'd feel if they got drunk on alcohol. They may also feel flushed and sweaty. Their hands and feet may lose feeling, and they'll be clumsy. Higher doses are more dangerous. High doses of PCP can cause nausea and vomiting. At high enough doses, people may have seizures. They could go into *comas*. They may die.

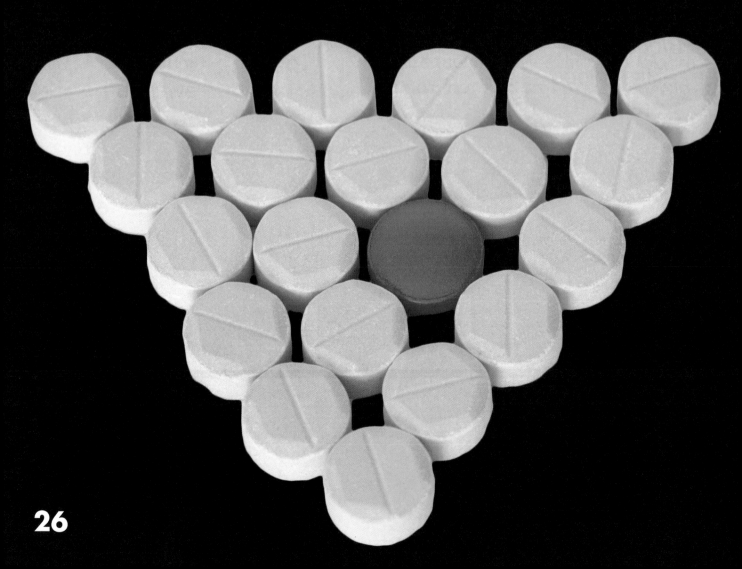

High doses of PCPs also make a person's eyes flick up and down uncontrollably.

The person who is high on PCP may drool and lose his balance. He may not be able to speak normally.

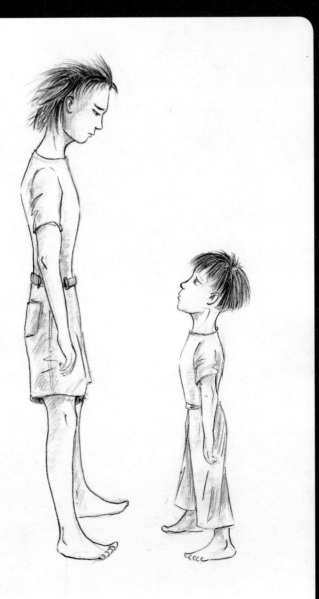

PCP use in teenagers can interfere with the *hormones* that trigger normal growth and development. This means teens may not mature normally.

10. WHAT HAPPENS TO YOUR BODY WHEN YOU USE HEROIN?

Short-term effects of

Heroin use has both short-term and long-term effects on the body. The short-term effects are what happen right after someone uses heroin. The long-term effects are what happen after a person has been using heroin over a long period of time.

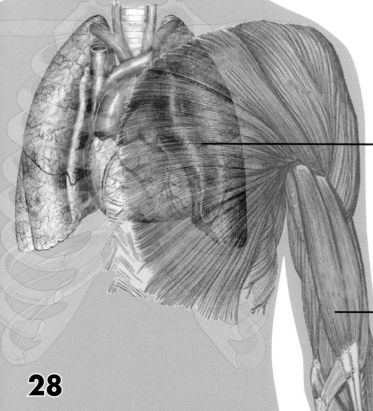

Mouth
- Dryness

Skin
- Warm flushing

Respiratory
- Slowed breathing

Muscular
- Weakness

People who use heroin many times over a long period of time have more serious effects. Their veins may collapse, and they may develop infections in their hearts and lungs. Their livers can be damaged. They may get sores (abscesses) all over their bodies.

The extra ingredients added to heroin can be as bad as the heroin itself. They can clog the blood vessels that lead to the lungs, liver, kidneys, and brain. They may contain poison.

When people share dirty needles for "shooting up" heroin, they pass along serious diseases to each other, including hepatitis and HIV, the virus that causes AIDS.

Long-term effects of
Heroin

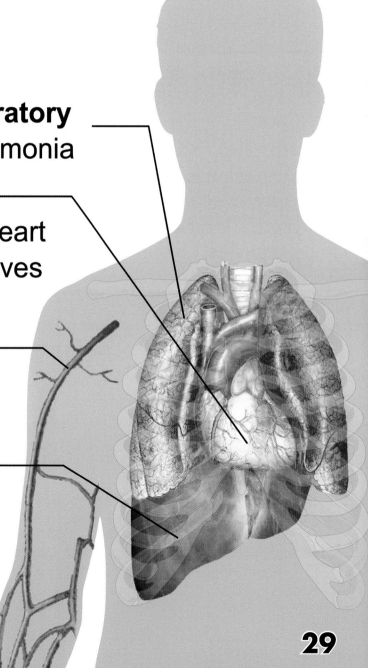

Respiratory
- Pneumonia

Heart
- Infection of heart lining and valves

Circulatory
- Collapsed veins

Liver
- Decreased function

Systemic
- Abscesses

11. HOW DOES COCAINE CHANGE YOUR BRAIN?

Smoking or injecting cocaine has almost immediate effects, and snorting it is nearly as fast. Cocaine quickly enters the bloodstream and travels to the brain. There it interferes with the chemicals that carry messages between the cells. It keeps these chemicals from being *reabsorbed* after they're released. When that happens, the chemicals build up in the brain. This makes the person feel "high."

He may have increased energy and alertness. He may feel very happy, and he may think he is better than anyone else.

Other people, though, have very different emotional reactions. They may feel angry at the world and restless. They may fear that everyone is out to get them. They may feel scared.

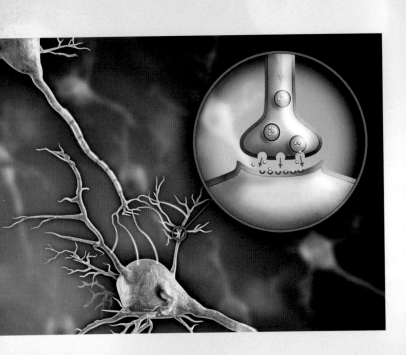

Scientists aren't exactly sure how LSD changes the brain—but they know that it changes serotonin. Serotonin is one of the chemicals that carries messages between brain cells. (Scientists calls these chemicals "neurotransmitters.") But LSD affects serotonin differently from what other drugs do. Scientists have discovered that LSD makes cells in certain regions of the brain become either more or less active. This changes the way a person sees the world.

LSD makes the person experience reality differently from what she does normally. She sees the "real" world around her—but in a different way. Things may seem to glow or move. They may be brightly colored.

He may feel as though he has a new understanding of God and reality. That's if he's having a "good trip." If he's having a "bad trip," he may be terrified by what he sees.

The LSD user might be able to "see" music or "hear" colors.

Some people believe that LSD stays in the brain, causing flashbacks. A "flashback" is when a person who has used LSD in the past has an experience, that's similar to a "trip"—without taking LSD. Scientists aren't sure what causes flashbacks, but some doctors think that that they're actually a form of mental illness that's brought on by LSD use.

People with histories of certain mental illnesses, such as *schizophrenia*, may get worse if they use LSD. LSD can also speed up the onset of mental illnesses in people who would probably have developed them anyway.

Heavy LSD users may not be able to sleep at normal times, and they may lose interest in eating. They may stop showering and changing their clothes. They may feel disconnected from the rest of the world. These feelings can get in the way of them being able to do well in school or at work. They can cause them problems in their relationships with friends and family.

13. HOW DOES PCP CHANGE YOUR BRAIN?

PCP is a sedative and a depressant, which means that it makes your brain and your body act more slowly (unlike cocaine, which is a stimulant that makes your brain and body function more quickly than normal).

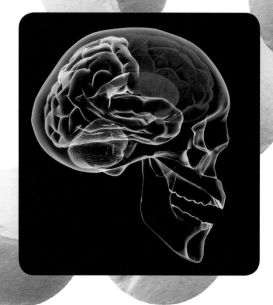

When a person is using PCP, his brain responds much like that of a person with schizophrenia. He won't be able to think or speak clearly. He may have delusions and *hallucinations*. He may feel *paranoid* and scared. Everything and everyone may seem very distant from him.

If someone combines PCP with other depressants—like alcohol, for example—the combined effect on the brain and body can slow things down so much that the person dies.

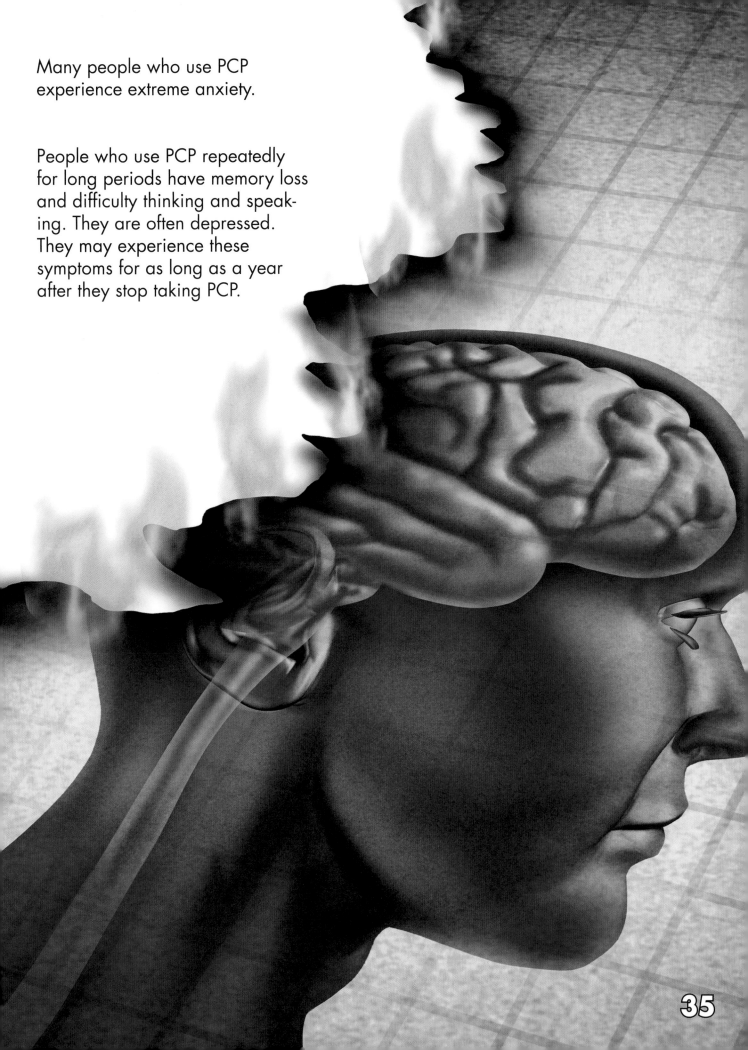

Many people who use PCP experience extreme anxiety.

People who use PCP repeatedly for long periods have memory loss and difficulty thinking and speaking. They are often depressed. They may experience these symptoms for as long as a year after they stop taking PCP.

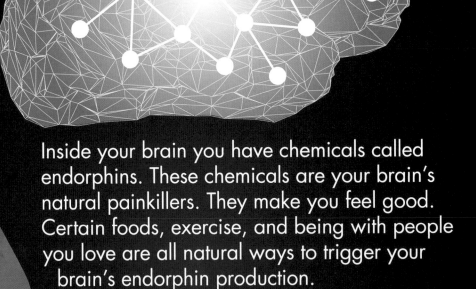

Inside your brain you have chemicals called
endorphins. These chemicals are your brain's
natural painkillers. They make you feel good.
Certain foods, exercise, and being with people
you love are all natural ways to trigger your
brain's endorphin production.

Heroin attaches to brain cells the same way
endorphins do. This makes users feel happy
at first—but after using heroin too many times,
their bodies stop producing endorphins on their
own. Now users can't feel good
without using heroin. Without
heroin, they'll feel depressed
and in pain.

People who use heroin have difficulty thinking clearly. They make decisions that don't make sense. They're not *motivated* to do much of anything.

Because heroin blocks the body's normal response to pain, people on heroin may hurt themselves without realizing what they've done.

Heroin can cause permanent brain damage. Users may experience memory loss and have a hard time learning new things. The parts of their brains needed to make decisions and solve problems may not work normally.

15. WHAT ARE THE LEGAL CONSEQUENCES OF USING HARD DRUGS?

Hard drugs and crime are often connected. Not only is it a crime to use, possess, manufacture, or distribute most hard drugs, using drugs can make people more likely to be violent. It can lower their *inhibitions* and affect their judgment, so that they break laws they wouldn't otherwise consider breaking.

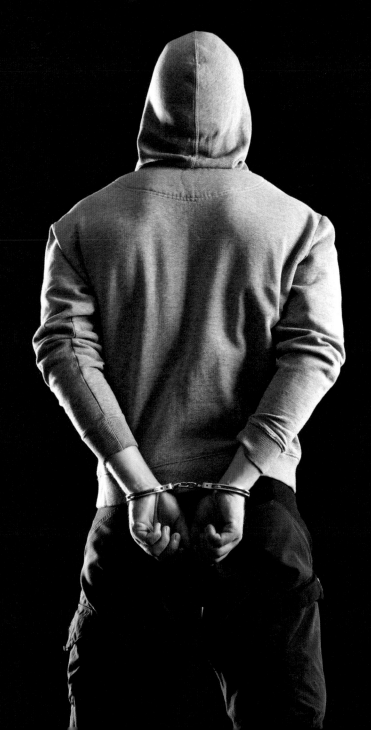

Drug trafficking—selling drugs—is an illegal form of business that often leads to many other forms of crime, from theft to murder.

Many hard drug users end up in prison. Hard drugs are a big problem inside prisons as well, where there is not enough treatment for inmates and hard drugs are often still available to them.

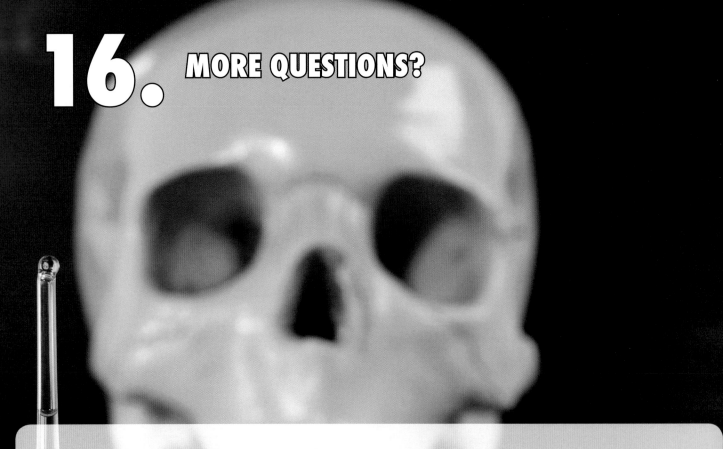

16. MORE QUESTIONS?

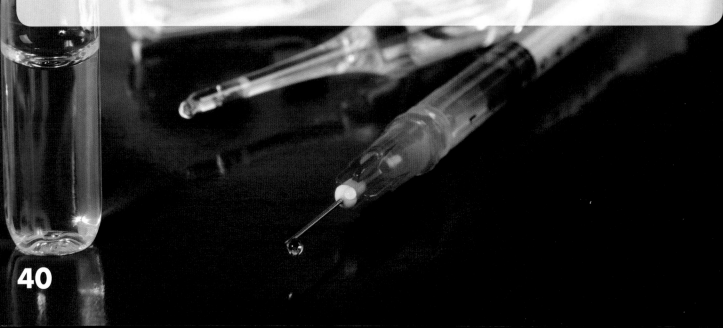

What should I do if I think someone has overdosed on a hard drug?

An overdose is when someone takes too much of any drug or medication, so that it causes serious, harmful symptoms or even death. If you think you or someone else has overdosed on a drug, you should always call 911 immediately. If it's not an emergency but you have questions about preventing an overdose, you can also call the National Poison Control Center (1-800-222-1222) from anywhere in the United States. It is a free call and it's *confidential*. You can call for any reason, 24/7.

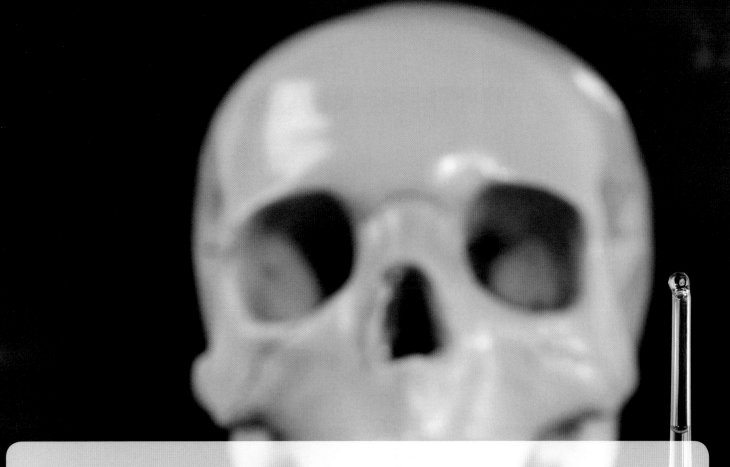

Can I use hard drugs and stay safe?

No, probably not. The only way to stay completely safe is not to use any of these drugs. The following practices make them even MORE risky:

- Mixing drugs, including alcohol, with any of these drugs increases the risk of overdose or death.
- Boosting (taking more of these drugs while already high) is even riskier.
- Taking these drugs alone or with people who might take advantage of you could put you in a dangerous situation. These drugs can affect your ability to recognize danger or make smart decisions.
- Driving a vehicle while using any of these drugs could kill you—or someone else.

FURTHER READING

Abadinsky, Howard. *Drug Use and Abuse*. Stamford, Conn.: Cengage, 2013.

Anonymous. *Go Ask Alice*. New York: Simon and Schuster, 2012.

Carlson, Dale. *Addiction: The Brain Disease*. Branford, Conn.: Bick, 2010.

Cobb, Allan B. *Heroin And Your Veins: The Incredibly Disgusting Story*. New York: Rosen, 2006.

Emmett, David. *Understanding Street Drugs*. London, UK: Jessica Kingsley, 2005.

Ferreiro, Carmen. *Heroin: The Straight Facts*. New York: Chelsea, 2003.

Jensen, Taylor S. *Cocaine: Understanding Drugs and Drug Addiction*. St. Louis, Mo.: JK Publishing, 2012.

Olive, M. Foster. *LSD: The Straight Facts*. New York: Chelsea, 2008.

Petechuk, David. *LSD*. San Diego, Calif.: Lucent, 2004.

Shelton, C. D. *Addiction: Understanding Addiction*. Harrison, Va.: Choice, 2013.

FIND OUT MORE ON THE INTERNET

Cocaine
www.nlm.nih.gov/medlineplus/cocaine.html

Cocaine Use and Its Effects
www.webmd.com/mental-health/cocaine-use-and-its-effects

Drug Effects: Heroin
www.drug-effects.com/heroineffects.htm

Drug Guide: PCP
www.drugfree.org/drug-guide/pcp

Hallucinogen Effects
www2.courtinfo.ca.gov/stopteendui/teens/resources/substances/hallucinogens/
short-and-long-term-effects.cfm

Heroin Abuse and Treatment
heroin.net

How LSD Works
www.howstuffworks.com/lsd.htm

Neuroscience for Kids: Heroin
faculty.washington.edu/chudler/hero.html

Neuroscience for Kids: PCP
faculty.washington.edu/chudler/pcp.html

Return of Angel Dust?
www.nbcnews.com/health/return-angel-dust-er-visits-linked-pcp-
spike-2005-2D11674428

GLOSSARY

anesthesia: Drugs used to put you to sleep or numb your sensation of pain during a medical procedure.

anxiety: A feeling of worry or fear.

coma: A deep unconsciousness that you can't wake up from.

confidential: Kept a secret.

delusional: Having beliefs that are not based in reality.

depression: A powerful feeling of sadness and hopelessness. It usually lasts a long time.

hallucinations: Things you see or hear that aren't really there.

hepatitis: A group of diseases that cause the liver to become inflamed or damaged.

hormones: Chemicals released in your body that affect how you grow, develop, and feel.

inhibitions: Feelings that stop you from acting in some way.

irrational: Not having a good reason.

irritates: Causes something to swell up and become inflamed.

insomnia: A condition where you have trouble falling or staying asleep.

motivated: Having a desire or reason to do something.

paranoid: Being afraid or suspicious without having a good reason to be.

reabsorbed: Took something back in.

schizophrenia: A psychological condition where a person loses touch with reality in some way.

seizures: Abnormal electrical activity in the brain that might cause muscle convulsions or unconsciousness.

stroke: A blocked or burst blood vessel in the brain that can cause brain damage.

symptoms: Signs or characteristics of a certain disease. For example, a fever might be a symptom of the flu.

tremors: Shaking of your muscles that you can't control.

ulcers: Sores that form inside your stomach or other organs.

INDEX

PICTURE CREDITS

ABOUT THE AUTHOR
AND THE CONSULTANT

CELICIA SCOTT lives in upstate New York. She worked in teaching before starting a second career as a writer.

JACK E. HENNINGFIELD, Ph.D., is a professor at the Johns Hopkins University School of Medicine, and he is also Vice President for Research and Health Policy at Pinney Associates, a consulting firm in Bethesda, Maryland, that specializes in science policy and regulatory issues concerning public health, medications development, and behavior-focused disease management. Dr. Henningfield has contributed information relating to addiction to numerous reports of the U.S. Surgeon General, the National Academy of Sciences, and the World Health Organization.